A Jarrold Area Guide
Written and compiled by **Reg Jones**

Birds of the Welsh Coast

Jarrold Colour Publications, Norwich

Introduction

The Welsh Coast extends for almost a thousand miles and includes a wide variety of habitats. There are towering cliffs which are often topped by steep slopes, flatter shores with shingle ridges and complex dune formations, and broad estuaries with sand banks and mud flats. In addition, there are many offshore islands ranging from uninhabited rocky stacks to one of the largest islands in Britain, Anglesey. Intermediate in size are Skomer, Skokholm, Ramsey and Bardsey, which are identified by Norse names and achieve a degree of remoteness by virtue of their separation from the mainland by stretches of sea which are often impassable.

With such variety it is not surprising to find thriving colonies of seabirds and other species particularly associated with the coast. Those which are situated on the cliffs and the islands escape disturbance because of the inaccessibility of the sites. Species which nest on more level ground are more at risk and usually owe their success to the safety offered within protected areas.

This booklet describes the commoner birds which can be seen around the Welsh Coast during the summer months.

Left: *Skomer from Skokholm.* **Above:** *Fulmar* ($\times\frac{1}{6}$).

The Fulmar nests on most coastal cliffs overlooking the sea. It is a relative newcomer, having established itself in Wales during the present century.

Although a fulmar may seem to resemble a gull, its wings are narrower, its neck is shorter and thicker, and the bill bears on its upper surface prominent tubular nostrils which are a feature of the petrel family to which the fulmar belongs. On land it can only shuffle awkwardly and finds difficulty in taking off from flat ground. In the air it is a master of the art of gliding, sweeping effortlessly along cliff faces on rigidly held wings, its tail often fanned, and banking steeply at the end of each sweep. The head, neck and under-parts are white in colour while the back and upper surface of the wings are pearly grey.

Fulmars are oceanic birds and those which nest in Britain range widely in the North Atlantic. They appear at their breeding stations as early as November and numbers build up steadily in the early part of the following year. The usual form of courtship display consists of birds sitting together on cliff ledges and, with necks extended, swinging their heads from side to side while producing a cackling 'ag-ag-ag-arr' from their gaping bills. Eggs are not laid before May. They are incubated for about 53 days and, since chicks are not airborne for a further seven or eight weeks after hatching, the cliffs are not deserted before late August or early September.

Above: *Manx Shearwater* ($\times\frac{1}{3}$).

Two other petrels are associated with the Welsh Coast. They are the Manx Shearwater and the Storm Petrel. Both visit the land during the hours of darkness, and the casual visitor is usually quite unaware of their presence.

The Manx shearwater is about 14 inches in length, black above and white underneath. Its wings are long and narrow and, like the fulmar, it is expert at gliding. It does not patrol cliff faces but rather skims over the surface of the sea, tilting from side to side as succeeding waves pass beneath it and exposing alternately its dark upper and light under-parts.

Manx shearwaters are rather helpless on land. Their legs lack the strength to fully support their bodies and they often fall forward to rest on their bellies. Probably because they are easy prey for the larger gulls, shearwaters only come ashore about two hours after sunset and often not at all on moonlit nights. As a preliminary to making a landfall, they assemble offshore in the evening and flocks or 'rafts' can be observed resting on the water.

Shearwaters nest in burrows, vast numbers often breeding in close proximity. On Skokholm, which is not a very large island, there are approximately 35,000 pairs. Skomer has an even larger population and on Bardsey there is a more modest colony of two or three thousand. A single egg is laid, usually in the first half of May, and this is incubated in turn by both parents, with an interval of about six days separating each change-over. During the day there is no sight or sound of a bird above ground, but at night sitting birds cackle and croon in their burrows and the air is filled with a babel of sound. As with the fulmar, there is a long incubation period of about 51 days and the chicks, which can only be fed at night, do not fly until they are, on average, ten weeks old.

Storm petrels are the smallest of European sea birds, being about 6 inches long. They are dark in colour except for a conspicuous white rump. Although they are long winged, they do not glide extensively but appear to flutter in an almost bat-like manner over the water, often with dangling feet.

The breeding biology of storm petrels is similar to that of shearwaters, single eggs being laid in rocky clefts, under boulders or in the recesses created within deteriorating dry-stone walls. Their nocturnal visits to land occur as soon as it is dark and moonlight does not deter them. Probably they are less prone to attack by predatory gulls since, on alighting, they do not linger for long on the ground before entering their nesting chambers. However, if little owls are present they can take a considerable toll.

Because of their habits, the presence of breeding storm petrels may be difficult to establish and the estimation of numbers even more so. Nevertheless, there is a colony of a few thousand pairs on Skokholm, smaller groups on Skomer, Middleholm and Bardsey, and probably other minor unrecorded gatherings elsewhere.

Below: *Storm Petrel* ($\times\frac{2}{5}$).

Above: *Gannet* ($\times\frac{1}{8}$).

The Gannet is the largest of British sea birds with a wing span of around 6 feet. It can often be observed in flight over the sea and at a distance appears glistening white in colour although at close quarters the long narrow wings are seen to be black tipped and the head and neck pale yellow. If the bird is fishing, it is unmistakable. Flying above the sea, suddenly it checks and then plunges headlong into the water with folded wings to reappear in a few seconds. A party of gannets circling over a shoal of fish and diving repeatedly provides an unforgettable spectacle.

Gannets are colonial birds, usually nesting in vast assemblages. The only sizable colony in England and Wales is at Grassholm, an island lying ten miles from the Pembrokeshire coast, where the numbers have built up from a few hundred pairs to more than 15,000 since the start of the century. Birds arrive at their breeding stations early in the year but eggs are not laid before April or May. Incubation lasts for at least six weeks and fledging takes as long as 90 days. With adults in attendance for most of the time, a gannetry is very much occupied until the early autumn.

Above: *Shags* ($\times\frac{1}{8}$).

Cormorants and Shags breed in colonies on rocky coastlines, the majority occurring in north-west Gwynedd, Anglesey and south-west Dyfed. Whereas in Britain, as a whole, shags greatly outnumber cormorants, in Wales the position is reversed with cormorants more than twice as numerous. The largest single colony is one of cormorants on St Margaret's Island with numbers of the order of 300 pairs.

Both species are dark in colour and have the same habit of standing on exposed rocks or breakwaters with wings outstretched. A shag's plumage has a green iridescence and adults in breeding dress possess distinctive upturned crests. Cormorants are rather larger birds, their feathers have a bronze cast and the cheeks and the upper part of the neck are white. In spring there is a light mark on the thigh which is conspicuous in flight.

Cormorants and shags are diving birds. The shag normally confines itself to deeper waters adjacent to rocky coasts. Cormorants often appear off low-lying shores, in shallow estuaries and in rivers where they take fish of commercial value and, as a result, are not popular with fishermen.

Left: *Male Shelduck* ($\times\frac{1}{6}$). **Lower right:** *Female Red-breasted Merganser* ($\times\frac{1}{5}$).

The Shelduck nests freely around the Welsh Coast in suitable habitats. It obtains most of its food from freshly exposed mud flats and naturally favours the flatter shores and broad tidal estuaries such as the Mawddach. At low water it can be seen walking slowly over the mud, swinging its bill from side to side, collecting the snails and worms contained within the wet surface layers.

Shelducks are large goose-like birds with distinctively variegated plumage. The white body is enlivened by a rufus collar around the breast and shoulders. There are bands of black and the dark green head terminates in a bright red bill which, in the male, is overhung at the base by a fleshy knob.

When breeding, shelducks usually nest out of sight in tunnel-like holes in sand dunes or beneath bramble cover on rough ground in the vicinity of the coast. After hatching, ducklings are led to the shore and family parties swimming on the water are common in high summer. Juveniles are brown-capped and banded and, unlike their parents, are active divers. By the end of July most of the adults are preparing to leave for the south-eastern corner of the North Sea where, on deserted sand banks, they can moult in comparative safety. Flotillas of young shelducks are left behind under the supervision of one or two mature birds.

A second duck, the Red-breasted Merganser, is a comparative newcomer. It is a species which has spread southwards from its more traditional haunts in Scotland and bred in Anglesey for the first time in 1953. Since then it has colonised suitable parts of the adjacent mainland and particularly the estuaries of Merioneth and Cardigan.

In summer, parties of young birds are seen on the water. They are accompanied by females and are recognisable by their slim brown heads which bear horizontal wispy crests. Their bills are elongated and toothed so as to be able to grasp fish under water. When feeding, families swim in line ahead with their heads almost immersed so that only their crests, standing stiffly erect, are visible. On sighting prey, the complete flotilla submerges as though by word of command.

Although primarily a woodland bird, the Buzzard also occurs in the mountains and on the coast where it breeds on ledges of precipitous sea-cliffs. Seaweed often forms a part of the nest.

Above: *Buzzard* ($\times\frac{1}{7}$). **Right:** *Peregrine* ($\times\frac{1}{3}$).

Buzzards are normally observed in the air where they are superb exponents of soaring flight. Hanging effortlessly on their broad wings, from the ends of which the flight feathers are splayed out like fingers, they glide and turn incessantly, often making good use of the draughts which sweep upwards from cliff faces. As they circle, they frequently call 'pee-oo'. From below, with a bird in silhouette against the sky, the head appears to be set well into the body so as to give a short-necked appearance and the tail, when expanded, is gently rounded.

Buzzards feed on small mammals, especially rabbits. The latter were plentiful until the advent of myxomatosis in the mid 1950s. Needless to say, there was a consequential fall in the buzzard population around 1956 which was followed by a gradual recovery, but to a lower level than previously. At present, buzzards are most likely to be seen about the rocky coastlines of south-west Dyfed and, to a lesser extent, of north-west Gwynedd.

The Peregrine Falcon is a true crag-nesting bird, usually laying its eggs on turfy platforms which are a feature of both inland cliffs and those overlooking the sea. In the 1930s it was relatively common around the Welsh

Coast but, unfortunately, the number has declined drastically since 1940. First, during the war, the bird was harried because of its habit of taking pigeons which were carrying war-time messages. Later with the large-scale use of agricultural pesticides; seed-eating birds, which often become the prey of peregrines, accumulated toxic residues within their tissues and these, in turn, were absorbed by the peregrines, causing death or infertility. Although this hazard is now somewhat reduced, the species is still threatened by egg-collectors and by falconers wanting young birds for training.

Nevertheless, it is still possible to come across the occasional peregrine resting on some rocky perch or to observe one in the air offshore. It is quite different from a buzzard with long scythe-like wings curving backwards to a point and with a tapering tail. It is not renowned for soaring but rather for its agility and, in particular, for the tremendous dives or 'stoops' which it makes at airborne prey, despatching them with slashing blows from its talons.

The Oystercatcher is a shore-nesting bird which breeds, wherever there are suitable sites, along most of the Welsh Coast. On open beaches, their eggs are inconspicuous against pebbly backgrounds. In more rocky places, clutches are placed in scrapes created between outcrops while occasionally nesting may take place on nearby grassy turf. Some of the largest concentrations occur on the island sanctuaries where there is less human interference.

Below: *Oystercatcher* ($\times\frac{1}{4}$).

Above: *Ringed Plover* ($\times\frac{1}{5}$).

The black and white plumage, together with orange-coloured bill and legs, make oystercatchers conspicuous at all seasons. Usually they feed by probing with their long bills in wet mud left uncovered at low water, seeking burrowing animals such as cockles. Where rocks abound, limpets are chipped from their anchorages and often nesting scrapes are then decorated with limpet shells. By high summer, oystercatchers are in parties which build up in number to form the massive flocks such as congregate about the Burry Inlet in winter.

The Ringed Plover favours those parts of the coast where shingle banks overlook tidal flats of mud and sand. Here it lays a typical plover clutch of four eggs which, being stone-coloured and speckled, are not readily distinguished from the surrounding pebbles. Unfortunately such areas, which occur on level shores, are subject to an appreciable amount of disturbance in summer and the bird has the best chance of breeding successfully in reserves such as Newborough Warren in Anglesey.

Ringed plovers run fitfully in short bursts over the ground. When halted, they bob nervously and call with a plaintive liquid note, 'too-ee'. Although the head and neck are patterned with black and white, the upper parts are sandy coloured which does not make the bird easy to pick out at a distance on the shore.

The oystercatcher and the ringed plover are wading birds. Four other members of the group which are more typical of inland habitats also nest by the coast. They are the Lapwing, Redshank, Curlew and Snipe.

Above: *Lapwing* ($\times\frac{2}{5}$). **Upper right:** *Redshank* ($\times\frac{1}{3}$).

Lapwings are usually regarded as birds of the moorlands and damp upland pastures. They also breed at lower levels. A number of pairs nest successfully on the wetter parts of the interior plateaux of Skomer and Skokholm while others occupy the 'morfas', areas of flat land adjacent to the coast which, over the years, have developed from storm beaches and are now covered by extensive dune formations which include wet slacks. Good examples are Morfa Dyffryn and Morfa Harlech.

The redshank often nests on similar ground to the lapwing, hiding its eggs within a tuft of grass or rushy clump rather than laying in an open scrape. It may also be found among the sand dunes. It is by no means widespread in its distribution, being absent as a breeding species in the south-western corner of Wales.

The curlew was formerly considered to be a species which bred on high ground but nowadays its wild call, 'cour-lee, cour-lee', is heard in springtime over many coastal flatlands. It is the largest of our wading birds and, apart from its size, the long curved bill allows for easy recognition. As early as July, when nesting is finished, small parties are common on estuarine mud flats at low water.

Common snipe normally nest in the wetter part of rushy marshes. They advertise their presence by indulging in sensational aerial displays, ascending to a good height before plunging earthwards with tails spread, the

Left: *Curlew* ($\times\frac{1}{5}$). **Right:** *Snipe* ($\times\frac{1}{3}$). **Lower right:** *Herring Gull* ($\times\frac{1}{5}$).

outermost feathers vibrating in the air to produce a tremulous hum which is referred to as drumming. In addition, when earthbound, snipe call continuously, 'chippa-chippa-chippa', and, when flushed, zigzag away uttering harsh 'scape's' as they go. Although obtaining much of their food by probing in soft mud, snipe seldom feed in the open like curlew, preferring boggy ground or the edges of standing water.

Gulls are the most familiar of coastal birds and, in Wales, the Herring Gull is the most numerous. Many thousands are present, breeding wherever there are cliffs or rocky islands offering comparatively safe nesting places. Sometimes they occupy flatter ground and occasionally, as in Newport Docks, take to roof-tops.

Herring gulls are easily recognised by their light grey mantles and wings, the ends of which are black with white tips. Their legs are flesh-coloured and their yellow bills carry a red flash on the lower mandible. They are great scavengers, hanging about harbours and picnic sites for scraps of food, and following boats at sea in the hope of picking up discarded trifles.

The herring gull is a relatively sedentary bird whereas the Lesser Black-backed Gull is primarily a summer visitor, the majority wintering in Portugal, southern Spain and north-western Africa. It is more powerfully built than a herring gull, the back and wings are slate-grey in colour and the legs are strikingly yellow.

Lesser black-backed gulls nest in large colonies, usually on more or less level ground. The most significant numbers occur in Anglesey, at Newborough Warren and on the Penmon Peninsula; on Skomer and Skok-

holm, where they are mainly on the island plateaux; and on Flatholm, an island in the Bristol Channel off Penarth.

The Great Black-backed Gull is the largest of the British gulls and, apart from its size is distinguished by its black upper-parts and flesh-coloured legs. In addition its call is deeper than those of other gulls, being a brief low-pitched bark, 'ag-ag-ag'.

Great black-backed gulls rarely breed together in considerable communities and, on the Welsh Coast, occur as small groups or solitary pairs which are often associated with large populations of other species. The nest is a simple depression lined with dry litter and is usually placed near a rocky prominence which can be used as a look-out. During the breeding season

Above: *Lesser Black-backed Gull* ($\times\frac{1}{6}$).

the adults are a menace to other sea birds, taking their eggs and young along with adult shearwaters and puffins.

The Black-headed Gull is the best known of British gulls to town-dwellers. In hard weather it descends on gardens to pick up household scraps and on the outskirts, haunts rubbish dumps, seeking edible garbage. In autumn and spring considerable flocks follow the plough, competing noisily for freshly uncovered earthworms and grubs. As the days lengthen, birds move to their breeding quarters which are often around inland lakes and pools where nests are built on islands or on tussocky clumps arising from waterlogged margins. Near the sea, black-headed gulls do not inhabit the cliffs, preferring lower level situations such as salt marshes, dunes and

Above: *Great Black-backed Gull* ($\times\frac{1}{7}$).

shingle banks. On the Welsh Coast, their numbers do not match those of the herring or lesser black-backed gulls, the largest colony at Morfa Harlech containing hundreds of pairs rather than thousands.

In breeding dress, the black-headed gull is unmistakable with its chocolate-brown head and blood-red bill and legs. From late July until the following spring, when the bird is most in evidence in towns, the head is white with darkness reduced to a smut behind the eye.

Kittiwakes are the daintiest of the gulls. They are oceanic birds, spending the autumn and winter in the North Atlantic. When breeding they still obtain their food from the sea and are rarely seen inland. Although as with other gulls they are grey and white in colour, their legs are black and the bill is uniformly pale yellow. In a colony, their oft repeated cry, 'kitt-ee-wake', is overwhelming in its intensity.

Above: *Black-headed Gull* ($\times\frac{1}{5}$). **Right:** *Kittiwake* ($\times\frac{1}{5}$).

Above: *Common Gull* ($\times\frac{1}{5}$).

Kittiwakes breed on sheer cliffs, placing their compact cup-shaped nests on the narrowest of ledges, often with open sea directly below. In Wales there are some 6,000–7,000 pairs. The most northerly colonies are on the Little Orme and the Great Orme, Llandudno, and the most southerly on the Worms Head, west Glamorgan. Between these two extreme positions there are several sizable gatherings on suitable cliff formations in Anglesey, north-west Gwynedd and south-west Dyfed, where, on Skomer, there is the largest single group.

The Common Gull, which is a widespread winter visitor, is largely confined to Scotland for breeding. However, in recent years, a few pairs have nested in Anglesey among colonies of herring gulls. While a common gull's plumage resembles that of a herring gull, in a mixed community the common gull is seen to be the smaller bird, its bill is much more slender and is greenish yellow, as are the legs. Its call is higher pitched than the familiar repetitive 'kyow-kyow' of the larger species.

Terns are summer visitors to Britain. They are more graceful than gulls. Their bodies are more slender, their wings are narrower and pointed, and the tail is usually forked. These features are responsible for them being referred to as 'sea-swallows'. At the coast, terns nest among sand dunes, on sand or shingle banks or on low-lying islets. In the twentieth century such places, and especially those on the mainland, have been subjected to increasing interference from holidaymakers and, as a result, in Wales numbers are relatively small.

The most abundant are Common and Arctic Terns which are largely confined to the western part of Anglesey. In appearance and behaviour the two species are very similar, often being referred to collectively as 'Comic Terns'. However, an arctic tern's bill lacks a black tip, its legs are shorter and its plumage is rather more dusky.

Colonies of common and arctic terns often include some Roseate Terns and also, occasionally, one or two pairs of Sandwich Terns. Roseate terns are about the same size as common and arctic but, on the ground, the legs are seen to be longer and the bill to be largely black. A pale rose-coloured tint on the breast in spring lasts for a very short time and usually birds appear to be much whiter than the other two species. In addition the tail streamers are very long, projecting well beyond the tips of the folded wings.

Sandwich terns are considerably larger in size. Their legs and bills are black, the latter ending in a yellow tip, and the dark feathers of the crown are elongated, producing a crest which makes the bird look irritable. All terns are volatile and noisy, and none more so than the sandwich tern.

The Little Tern is markedly smaller than those already mentioned, being not much more than 8 inches in length. Apart from size, it is distinguished

Below: *Common Tern* ($\times\frac{2}{7}$).

in summer by a white forehead to the black crown together with a yellow bill and legs. Little terns breed in diffuse groups, the majority of their nests being placed just above the high-water mark. They compete with man for space and, regrettably, only a few pairs now occur along the coastline extending northwards from the district of Meirionnydd in Gwynedd.

Three members of the Auk family occur in good numbers on cliff-girded coasts: the Razorbill, the Guillemot and the Puffin. A fourth, the Black Guillemot, is represented by a very few birds in one area.

Razorbills are so named because of the compressed shape of their bills. As with other auks, the wings are short and beat rapidly to produce a whirring, direct type of flight. On land they are almost penguin-like. Floating on the water beneath their breeding cliffs, they appear plump and compact, and hold their bills and tails in stiffly angled positions. Usually they nest out of sight in a crevice or under a boulder.

A guillemot is slightly larger than a razorbill but much slimmer in build, and the darker parts are dark brown rather than black. Birds nest close together on narrow ledges, standing side by side, their heads forever on the move on twisting, sinuous necks. They are the noisiest of the auks, growling, 'arrr', almost continuously.

Above: *Little Tern* ($\times\frac{1}{2}$).

Above: *Razorbill* ($\times\frac{2}{5}$).

Razorbills and guillemots are diving birds, their food consisting of small fish, such as sand-eels, and other marine life. In both species single eggs are laid and incubated for about five weeks. Their chicks are fed on fish which is brought ashore by the parents, but the young are remarkable in that they flutter down to the sea when they are not much more than two and a half weeks old and barely one third the size of the adults. Though their development is far from complete, they can swim and dive effectively and they are escorted to sea by the parent birds.

Being restricted to cliffs, razorbills and guillemots are commonest in south-west Dyfed and north-west Gwynedd. Smaller numbers can be seen elsewhere, some of the more familiar places being Worms Head, west Glamorgan; Bird Rock, south of New Quay, Dyfed; South Stack, Holyhead, Anglesey. Guillemots outnumber razorbills by three to one.

Black guillemots are more characteristic of northern latitudes but since 1962 a few pairs have bred in Anglesey. In nuptial dress, they are sooty-black with contrasting white wing patches and red feet. They differ from common guillemots in laying two eggs which are placed under rocks or within cliff holes, and, as a rule, not far above the high-tide mark.

Puffins have the black and white plumage of auks but, in spring, because of their large triangular, multi-coloured bills, they cannot be confused with any other species. Although some eggs, like those of razorbills, are hidden in crevices or under boulders, many are laid in burrows excavated in the grassy turf covering the upper parts of cliffs or low-lying islands. A puffin produces a single egg about the end of April; this early date, no doubt, being associated with a lengthy incubation period of around six weeks, after which a further seven weeks elapses before the fully fledged youngster leaves its shelter, often under the cover of darkness, for the sea.

There are fewer colonies of puffins on the Welsh Coast than of razorbills and guillemots. The most substantial are on Skomer and Skokholm in Dyfed. Farther north, there are smaller groups in Anglesey, including the South Stack, and on Gwylan-Fawr, off Aberdaron in Gwynedd.

Jackdaws are common where there are coastal cliffs, occurring in small flocks which nest communally. Flying together, they chatter with high-pitched 'tchacks'. Close at hand, they can be seen to be smaller than crows

Left: *Guillemots* ($\times\frac{1}{6}$).
Right: *Black Guillemot* ($\times\frac{1}{4}$).

and, although they are mainly black in colour, the nape of the neck and the cheeks are grey. They feed on small animals taken from the ground and sometimes take the eggs and young of other birds.

The Welsh Coast is a main stronghold of the Raven, which is the largest of the crows. Often it can be seen in the air, soaring freely, its tail distinctly wedged. In spring, it performs aerobatics, executing complicated rolls and dives, and at all times its deep-throated call, 'pruk-pruk', is distinctive.

Ravens breed as solitary pairs, constructing substantial nests on rocky ledges. Eggs are laid as early as February and by late summer, with nesting completed, birds often congregate in parties for roosting. Their food includes carrion.

Because of its rarity elsewhere in Britain, the Chough is of special interest. Small numbers are present and are most likely to be seen along the Lleyn Peninsula or in the south-west of Dyfed. They are slightly larger than jackdaws, but are more uniformly dark in colour and are especially distinguished by their long and curved red bills and legs. Except in the breeding season, when individual pairs nest in sea caves and similar inaccessible chambers, they are social although parties are never large in number. In the air, they proceed in a leisurely manner, flapping and gliding on broad wings. On the ground, where there is soft turf, their slender bills are used for probing for grubs and worms.

Left: *Puffin* ($\times\frac{1}{4}$).
Below: *Raven* ($\times\frac{1}{7}$).
Right: *Chough* ($\times\frac{1}{7}$).

Below: *Jackdaw* ($\times\frac{1}{3}$).

Above: *Male Wheatear* ($\times\frac{2}{3}$).

Several small land-based birds occur around the coastline. Wheatears are summer visitors arriving about mid-March. They are easily identified by their white rumps, which are visible as they flit from one perch to another. In breeding dress the male has light grey upper parts whereas the hen is more sandy brown.

Wheatears require small hidden cavities within which to nest. Disused rabbit holes or niches beneath rocks are often used. These are more likely to occur on the slopes capping steep cliffs than on sheer cliff faces. The

Above: *Male Stonechat* ($\times\frac{3}{4}$).

bird is most numerous on offshore islands.

Stonechats are present throughout the year and are characteristic of those areas where gorse is particularly abundant. Nests are usually built on the ground in thick cover at the foot of a furze bush. As with wheatears, stonechats feed, in the main, on insects and the most common sighting is of a cock bird perching on a spring of gorse, flicking and flirting its wings and tail, its bill crammed with food. The head and tail are dark in colour, and the breast light chestnut. It scolds with a harsh 'tsak-tsak'.

Above: *Rock Pipit* ($\times\frac{1}{3}$).

The small lark-like birds which can be seen flitting from one rocky crag to another on cliff faces are Rock Pipits. In summer they are restricted to rock-bound coasts and hide their nests in clefts or among the clumps of thrift and campion covering cliff ledges. They are smaller than skylarks, their plumage is similarly streaked yet darker in tone. Their legs are almost black and the outer tail feathers lack the pure whiteness evident in the skylark and the meadow pipit, a paler coloured relative which is often common on rough pasture adjacent to the cliff tops.

Rock pipits disperse when the nesting season is over and some birds can then be seen on flatter shores often searching among the litter cast up along the high-tide line for flies and sand hoppers.